ADAPTATION

Holly Wallace

www.heinemann.co.uk
Visit our website to find out more information about Heinemann Library books.

To order:
 Phone 44 (0) 1865 888066
Send a fax to 44 (0) 1865 314091
 Visit the Heinemann Bookshop at www.heinemann.co.uk to browse our catalogue and order online.

First published in Great Britain by Heinemann Library, Halley Court, Jordan Hill, Oxford OX2 8EJ a division of Reed Educational and Professional Publishing Ltd. Heinemann is a registered trademark of Reed Educational & Professional Publishing Ltd.

OXFORD MELBOURNE AUCKLAND
JOHANNESBURG BLANTYRE GABORONE
IBADAN PORTSMOUTH (NH) USA CHICAGO

Designed by Celia Floyd
Originated by Dot Gradations
Printed in Hong Kong/China

ISBN 0 431 10922 2
05 04 03 02 01
10 9 8 7 6 5 4 3 2 1

British Library Cataloguing in Publication Data

Wallace, Holly
 Adaptation. - (Living things)
 1. Adaptation (Biology) - Juvenile literature
 I. Title
 578.4

Acknowledgements

The Publishers would like to thank the following for permission to reproduce photographs:

Bruce Coleman Collection: Mary Plage pg.14; *Corbis*: Daniel Samuel Robbins pg.9; *NHPA*: pg.20, NA Callow pg.4, David Middleton pg.4, A.N.T. pg.7, pg.24, Darek Karp pg.8, Stephen Dalton pg.10, pg.16, pg.28, Anthony Bannister pg.11, pg.25, Martin Harvey pg.12, pg.15, Dr Eckart Pott pg.13, Hellio & Van Ingen pg.17, GJ Cambridge pg.18, EA Janes pg.19, Roy Waller pg.19, Norbert Wu pg.21, B & C Alexander pg.22, John Shaw pg.23, Daniel Heuclin pg.25, David Hosking pg.27, Vincente Gardia Canseco pg.29; *Oxford Scientific Films*: Daniel J Cox pg.4, Colin Milkins pg.6, Michael Fogden pg.10, Richard Herrmann pg.20, Roland Mayr pg.26, Sean Morris pg.27.

Cover photograph reproduced with permission of NHPA.

Every effort has been made to contact copyright holders of any material reproduced in this book. Any omissions will be rectified in subsequent printings if notice is given to the Publisher.

Any words appearing in the text in bold, **like this**, are explained in the glossary.

Contents

Many habitats 4

Changing conditions 6

Life in the mountains 8

In the forest 10

Rolling grasslands 12

Flowing waters 14

Lakes and ponds 16

Tides and waves 18

Life in the ocean 20

Life at the poles 22

Heat and drought 24

Extreme habitats 26

In the city 28

Glossary 30

Index 32

Introduction

The six books in this series explore the world of living things. *Adaptation* looks at how plants and animals have developed special features that help them to survive in a particular place. These features are called adaptations.

Many habitats

The place where plants and animals live is called a **habitat**. There are many different habitats in the world, such as mountains, lakes, woods and seashores. Most living things are **adapted** to life in one particular habitat. They would not be able to survive anywhere else.

A dolphin's shape is designed for sliding through the water.

Seas and deserts

A dolphin is adapted to life in the sea. It has a smooth, **streamlined** body for swimming. A camel is adapted to life in the hot, dry desert. Neither animal could survive in the other's habitat.

These little shieldbugs live in the garden. Their colours match their surroundings. This makes them harder for hungry enemies to spot and eat.

Survival needs

Living things live in places that provide what they need to survive. This includes:

- Food. All living things need food to stay alive. Food gives them energy to make new **cells**, grow and stay healthy.
- **Oxygen**. Living things need oxygen to release energy from their food. They get oxygen from the air.
- Water. Water is vital for keeping the cells of a plant or animal in good working order.
- Shelter. Living things need shelter from the weather and from **predators** that hunt them for food.
- A **mate** for **breeding**. Living things must **reproduce** to replace those that die.

This book shows how living things have adapted to find the things they need.

Coniferous trees on cold mountainsides provide shelter and food for some animals.

On the move

Some animals have special features to help them survive in their habitat. For example:

- A fish has fins for pushing through the water.
- A bird has wings for flying through the air.
- A mole has strong front paws for burrowing in soil.
- A monkey has long arms for swinging through the trees.

Changing conditions

Conditions in a **habitat** change from day to day. The Sun rises and sets. The weather brings rain, wind and snow. The seasons change throughout the year. Along the seashore, the tide rises and falls. Living things must cope with the changing conditions if they are to survive.

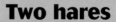

A **barnacle's** life is ruled by the rise and fall of the tides (see page 18).

Hot and cold

Every day, the Sun rises and sets. In many places, this brings warm days and cool nights. Many animals, such as snakes, are **cold-blooded**. They rely on the surrounding temperature to warm up or cool down. At night, snakes are sluggish and slow. They have to warm up in the morning Sun so that they can move fast and chase their **prey**. As night falls again, many snakes slither under a rock to rest and hide.

Two hares

Some very similar animals have **adapted** to life in very different places around the world:
- The African hare has long legs and ears, and short fur. These help it lose heat and keep cool in its hot, desert home.
- The Arctic hare has short legs and ears, and long, thick fur. These features help keep it warm in its icy cold home.

Life in the dark

Some animals are **nocturnal**. This means that they come out at night to look for food. They include moths, mice, owls and bats. They have special features, such as large eyes and ears, for finding food and their way in the dark.

Mice have huge eyes, long whiskers and sensitive noses for finding their way in the dark.

Special features

- Body shape – A worm is long and thin for burrowing through the soil. A leaf is broad and flat to catch sunlight. (Plants use sunlight to make their food.)
- Colour and pattern – A green tree frog's markings make it tricky to see among the green leaves. This helps to hide it from its enemies.
- Body parts – A snake has long, pointed fangs for stabbing poison into its prey. A beaver has sharp teeth for cutting wood.

Similar features

Some very different animals have adapted to life in the same place:
- Frogs, lizards and squirrels that live in trees have long, thin fingers for grasping the branches.
- Frogs, lizards and squirrels that live on the ground have short, stubby fingers for walking and running.

Life in the mountains

The higher you go up a mountain, the colder it gets. This is why very high mountains are topped with ice and snow. Strong, freezing winds howl and blow. There is also less **oxygen** to breathe. Despite the harsh conditions, many hardy plants and animals have **adapted** to life on steep mountainsides all over the world.

Mountain animals

Mountain animals, such as **vicuñas** and yaks, have very long, thick fur to keep them warm. Mountain goats have sharp-edged hooves for keeping their footing on the slippery slopes. Even at the very top of some mountains, you find tiny insects and spiders. They feed on the bodies of dead plants and animals, blown up by the wind.

Did you know?
● Yaks have the longest fur of any **mammals**. It grows up to 1 metre long.
● Plants, such as pasque flowers, have hairy leaves to keep out the cold.

An alpine pasque flower with its furry leaves.

Up and down

Some animals, like yaks and goats, spend summer high up on the mountainside. They graze on the plants that grow in the grassy meadows. In autumn, they go back down the mountain to keep out of the winter cold.

Yaks live high up in the Himalaya mountains in Asia.

Mountain plants

Different plants live at different heights on the mountain. This is because the weather changes as you climb higher up. The lower slopes are warmer and more sheltered. Here you get rainforests or **deciduous** forests, depending on which part of the world you are in. Many animals live here. Then you get **coniferous** trees that can cope well with the snow and wind.

The tree line

Next comes the tree line. Trees cannot live above this point. It is too cold and windy for them to grow. Above the tree line are grassy meadows. Here the plants are short and low-growing to keep out of the wind. Higher still are icy rocks and crags where no plants can grow.

In the forest

Rainforests are the richest **habitats** on Earth. They are home to millions of different plants and animals. This is because they are warm and wet all year round, the perfect conditions for living things. But there are other kinds of forest around the world where life is much tougher.

Rainforest life

The rainforest is bursting with life, in all shapes, sizes and colours. Plants and animals do not have to struggle to find warmth or water. But so many of them live in one place that they have to **compete** with each other for space, shelter and food. So they use sounds and colours to warn others to keep out of their way.

A macaw squawks loudly to warn other birds away from its rainforest home.

The forest floor is dark and gloomy. So some rainforest plants, like **bromeliads**, grow high in the trees near the light.

Winter cold

In forests growing in colder places, winter is tough for animals. Apart from the cold, there is very little food to eat. Some animals, such as dormice, survive by **hibernating** until spring. Squirrels rest in their nests. Sometimes they come out to dig up nuts they buried in the autumn. Some birds, such as swifts, fly away to warmer places. This is called **migration**. They will return to the forest in the spring.

Frozen solid

In the far north, winters are even colder and longer. **Coniferous** trees, such as firs and spruces, have special features for coping with the cold. Their branches slope down so that snow slides off and does not break the branches. Some animals have amazing ways of surviving. The Siberian salamander freezes almost solid. Then it thaws out in the spring.

Hiding in the forest

Many forest animals have special colours and markings to hide from enemies or catch their **prey** by surprise. These are called **camouflage**.

- Stick insects look like thin, brown twigs.
- Thornbugs are shaped like sharp tree thorns.
- Moths look like old dead leaves on the forest floor.
- Spiders have bright colours to look like tropical flowers.

This twig is actually a caterpillar. It stays quite still while there is danger about.

Rolling grasslands

Huge, rolling **grasslands** grow in many parts of the world. There is not enough rain for trees to survive but many tough grasses and bushes can grow. Grassland animals have to cope with the lack of shade and shelter in the long, dry season, then with sudden floods when the rains come.

Grassland animals, such as giraffes and antelope, have long legs for running away from enemies.

The Prairies

In North America, the grasslands are called prairies. Here the biggest animals are bison. They graze on the grass and have wide, flat teeth for chewing. Their huge size helps to protect them from enemies, such as hungry wolves. This is also why they live together in large herds. In Africa the grasslands are called savannah. Herds of zebra and wildebeest live here.

Big birds

Grasslands are home to the world's biggest birds. Ostriches live in Africa, emus in Australia and rheas in South America. These birds cannot fly. But they all have long, powerful legs and can run very fast to escape from their enemies. They can also kick very hard!

Living in burrows

Many small grassland animals dig burrows and tunnels where they hide from their enemies. In North America, prairie dogs build huge underground towns. Some prairie dogs act as guards and look out for danger. If a fox or hawk comes near, they yap and bark a warning. Then the other prairie dogs can hurry to safety underground.

Dung beetles collect **dung** from grassland **mammals**. They use it as food for their grubs.

Termite cities

Termites are tiny insects that would soon die in the hot Sun. So they build a huge mound of mud that dries hard. Then they dig a huge nest underneath. Here a million or more termites live together in a cool underground city.

Did you know?

Some grassland plants and animals help each other, such as acacia trees and ants. The ants bite and sting animals who try to eat the tree's leaves. In return, they get a safe place to live among the tree's sharp thorns.

Flowing waters

Each part of a river provides a different **habitat**. At first, the river flows fast downhill. Then it slows down over the plains. Sand and mud collect along its banks. Finally, it flows into the sea at its mouth or **estuary**. Here the fresh river water mixes with the salty water of the sea. Many different plants and animals are **adapted** to life in different parts of the river.

Fast flowing

At first, the river flows so fast that it sweeps most plants and animals away. But some animals can survive in these conditions. Stonefly grubs, for example, have strong claws for gripping the pebbles on the river bottom.

This bird called a dipper dives for food in a fast-flowing river.

Slowing down

As the river slows down, mud collects on its banks and bottom. Plants, such as reeds and rushes, take root in the mud. They provide food and shelter for many animals. Fish, such as perch and pike, lurk among the reeds. They hunt fish, insects and worms for food.

Into the sea

At the river's mouth, fresh water mixes with the salty sea. Salt can kill freshwater animals by poisoning their **cells**. Some animals are adapted to live in both salt water and fresh water. They include fish, such as salmon and mullet, and shellfish, such as mussels and oysters.

Mangrove swamps

Mangrove trees grow in huge muddy swamps where tropical rivers flow into the sea. They have long, tangled roots for anchoring them in the shifting mud. They get rid of waste salt through their leaves. Otherwise the salt could kill them.

Beaver homes

Beavers have large front teeth for gnawing down trees. They build a wooden **dam** across a stream to form a pond. In the pond, they build a wooden **lodge** to live in. The lodge is safe from enemies, such as wolves and coyotes.

Sharks and rays swim into sheltered mangrove swamps to lay their eggs.

Did you know?

The saltwater crocodile is the biggest **reptile** in the world. It grows more than 8 metres long. It lives in estuaries and mangrove swamps around the Indian and Pacific Oceans.

Lakes and ponds

A lake or pond does not have the problems of fast-flowing water. But if the water is warm and still, it contains less **oxygen**. Fish and other lake creatures need to breathe oxygen to stay alive. Many get their oxygen from the water. But getting a good enough supply can be difficult.

The rat-tailed maggot uses its tail like a snorkel to breathe in air.

Breathing

Lungfish have **gills** that absorb oxygen from water. They also have body parts like lungs. When there is not enough oxygen in the water, they can breathe air.

Tubes and bubbles

Some other lake and pond creatures have clever ways of getting enough oxygen. The rat-tailed maggot is the **larva** of the hoverfly. It lives in still, shallow water. It breathes through its tube-like tail. It can extend its tail 15 centimetres to reach the surface air.

Many diving beetles live underwater but visit the surface for air. They trap bubbles of air on their bodies and store it for later.

The water in ponds and creeks is often cloudy and muddy. It is difficult for animals to see to hunt their prey. The platypus from Australia uses its duck-like beak to dig around in the mud for worms, shellfish and insects.

Did you know?

The electric eel lives in South America. It uses an electric shock to stun its prey of fish and frogs, and scare away its enemies.

Upside-down beaks

Flamingoes live around lakes in warm parts of the world. They eat tiny shrimps and plants. They use their curved beaks like sieves to strain food out of the water. They hold their beaks upside-down and suck water in. Then they push the water out with their tongues, leaving their food behind.

Hunting for food

The top hunters in lakes and swamps are crocodiles and alligators. They lie just under the water, looking out for **prey**. They have nostrils and eyes on top of their heads so that they can still see, smell and breathe. Then they grab their prey with their long jaws and sharp teeth.

A flamingo's beak is **adapted** for sieving its food out of the water.

17

Tides and waves

Coasts and seashores are always changing. Twice a day, the sea rises and floods the shore with salty water. Then the sea flows out again. These changes in sea-level are called the tides.

This makes life difficult for many living things. At high tide, plants and animals are swamped by the waves and may be swept out to sea. At low tide, they are in danger of drying out in the Sun and wind.

Shore-fish, like blennies, have tough, rubbery skin to protect them from the waves.

Tough plants

Seaweeds are plants that grow along the seashore. They do not have proper roots like plants on land. But many have strong, root-like **holdfasts** that cling to the rocks. This stops the seaweed being swept away by the waves. They also have tough, leaf-like **fronds** with slippery surfaces. They are not torn by waves or dried out by the Sun. Some seaweeds are enormous. Their fronds grow many metres long.

Hiding away

Many seashore animals hide away at low tide. At high tide, they become more active. Some animals, such as crabs and sea-snails, come out to find food. Others, such as cockles and clams, shelter under the mud or sand. When the tide comes in, they stick up tiny tubes. They suck in water through one tube. They sieve food from the water, then squirt the water out through the other tube. Many animals hide away at low tide so that their bodies do not dry out. They swim away when the tide comes in.

When the tide comes in, sea anemones catch food with their tentacles. At low tide, they curl up.

A crab sheltering among the seaweed at low tide.

Shore birds

At low tide, birds gather on the shore to look for food. Many, such as dunlins and oystercatchers, have long, pointed bills for probing the sand in search of shellfish, snails, worms and crabs to eat.

Did you know?

Lugworms dig burrows in the sand. They eat the sand to get tiny bits of food. Then they push the rest of the sand to the surface as a wiggly **worm cast**.

Lif in the ocean

The oceans are the biggest **habitat** on Earth. They are bigger than all the other habitats put together. A huge number of living things survive in the sea. Some live in the shallow water near the coast, or in the open ocean. Others live deep down, where the water is dark and freezing cold.

Sealions swim and feed off the warm coast of California.

Big fish

The biggest fish in the sea is the whale shark. It grows over 18 metres long and weighs 20 tonnes. But it is **adapted** for feeding on tiny sea creatures called plankton. Plankton are too small to see with your eye. It sieves them from the seawater using frilly combs in the sides of its head.

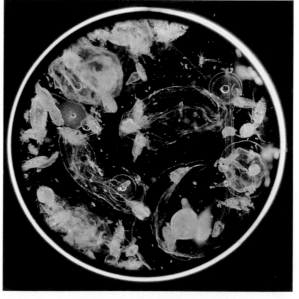

Huge whale sharks eat tiny sea creatures like these.

Deep divers

Sperm whales are **mammals**. This means that they have to come to the surface to breathe air. But they eat deep-sea sharks and squid. Luckily, sperm whales can hold their breath for almost two hours so they can dive deep for food. They have a waxy substance in their foreheads. This gets heavier as they dive, helping them to go deeper. A sperm whale can dive deeper than 3000 metres.

The deep-sea bed

The deep sea is cold and dark. No sunlight can reach this far down. Many deep-sea creatures, such as clams and sea cucumbers, are blind. They do not have eyes because there is no light to see. Instead, they have sensitive bodies for feeling their way in the dark. They eat tiny pieces of food that drift down from the surface and settle on the seabed.

Finding food

Finding food is difficult in the deep sea. So fish have to make the most of any food they find. Gulper eels have huge mouths and stomachs for swallowing **prey** much bigger than themselves.

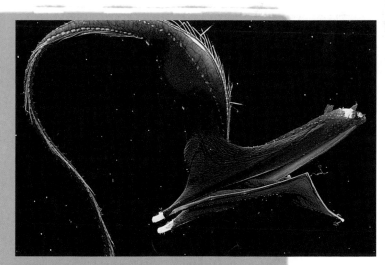

A gulper eel showing its huge mouth.

Life at the poles

Near the North and South **Poles**, life is very harsh indeed. Even the sea freezes and the land is covered in ice and snow. Living things have to cope with the icy cold, howling winds, short summers and long, dark winters. It seems that nothing could live in these freezing places. But some plants and animals have special features and skills that help them survive.

Reindeer graze on **lichens** and short grasses that they dig out of the snow. Herds of reindeer walk long distances to find enough food.

Summer and winter

At the poles, summers are very short. But it is light all day and night and the temperature rises above freezing. So living things can survive. But winters are very long and dark. Then the temperature can fall to below minus 50 °C, too cold for living things.

Summer visitors

Many Arctic birds, such as ducks and geese, fly south to warmer places for the winter to find food. Otherwise they would not survive. They fly north again in the spring to build their nests and raise their young.

Plants

Plants near the poles must make the most of the short summer time. They bloom quickly and scatter their seeds which will grow into new plants. Plants grow close to the ground to keep out of the wind.

Warm coats

Arctic animals include polar bears, snowshoe hares and snowy owls. They have thick coats of fur or feathers for keeping warm. They also have a thick, warm layer of fat under their skin. Many spend the winter in caves, burrows and dens.

Some Arctic animals change colour in the winter. Their coats turn white to match the snow. In summer they turn brown to match the ground. This helps to hide them from their enemies.

Ptarmigan have white feathers in winter and brown feathers in summer for camouflage.

Ice-cold seas

The seas around Antarctica are icy cold. But they are also rich in tiny sea plants and animals. These provide food for small fish and shrimps. Bigger fish, penguins, seals and whales eat the smaller creatures.

Did you know?
Tiny insects called springtails live on land in icy Antarctica all year round. They have special **chemicals** in their blood to stop them freezing.

Heat and drought

Some deserts are sandy or rocky. Some are hot all year round or cold in winter. Many are baking hot by day and freezing cold at night. But all deserts have one thing in common. They are the driest places on Earth. Some deserts do not get any rain for months or years on end.

Desert frogs

The water-holding frog lives in the Australian desert. When it rains, the frog drinks so much water that it blows up like a small balloon. Then it hides in its underground burrow. It uses the water in its store until the next rains come. Then thousands of frogs suddenly appear.

Desert plants

For most of the time, deserts look dry and dead. But as soon as it rains, the desert bursts into bloom. Millions of seeds are buried underground. When it rains, they sprout very quickly

A water-holding frog can survive long periods of drought.

and grow flowers and seeds. Then these seeds lie in the ground until the next rain shower.

Many desert animals get water from the plants they eat. So plants have to protect their juicy leaves and stems. Cacti do not have leaves. They have sharp spines instead. These help keep thirsty creatures away.

The darkling beetle stands on its head and catches dew on its back legs. Then the dew trickles into its mouth.

Cool burrows

Many small desert animals, such as gerbils and kangaroo rats, hide from the daytime heat. They spend the day in underground burrows. Here the temperature is much cooler than above. The animals come out at night to find food.

Shifting sands

It can be difficult to move across soft desert sand. It is always sliding and slipping. Many desert animals have special features to help them get about:

- Kangaroo rats and gerbils have large back feet for hopping and jumping.
- Camels have wide feet to stop them sinking in the sand.
- Some desert lizards wriggle through the sand, like fish swimming through water.

Camels in the Sahara Desert.

Extreme habitats

Some places on Earth seem so harsh that it is difficult to see how livings things could survive there. They include ice-cold glaciers and icebergs, volcanic islands, boiling hot springs, deep, dark caves and places that have been burned by fires. But even here, living things have found ways of staying alive. They do not have many rivals for space and food. So some animals survive in large numbers.

Surviving a fire

After a bush fire, the earth is ashy and black. It seems that nothing could grow in it. But some plants grow very quickly. They scatter their seeds, then die off before other plants take their place. Some trees have tough, thick bark that does not get damaged in the fire. Some plants have roots and other parts underground. They also survive the scorching.

Plants shooting up after a fire in Yellowstone National Park, USA.

Did you know?

In 1963, a new island called Surtsey appeared in the sea near Iceland. At first, it was bare rock. But lots of plants and animals now live there.

New land

Surtsey was made by a volcano erupting under the water. But how did the plants and animals get there? The wind blew some plant seeds over. Birds visited the island and brought animal eggs and plant seeds in their feathers and droppings. Tiny **mites** and spiders were also carried by the wind. Soon the island was covered in life. Now more than 1000 **species** of plants and animals live there.

Hot and cold

Some living things can survive scorching heat. The water in some hot springs is too scalding to touch. But tiny **bacteria** and **algae** grow and form crusts on the rocks. Other living things can survive freezing cold. Some types of bacteria live on the undersides of icebergs. In Alaska, tough ice-worms burrow through the ice.

Bacteria and algae grow in these hot springs in North America.

In the city

A bustling big city might seem like a dangerous place to live. There are lots of people, noise and traffic. But many animals move into cities because their wild **habitats** are being destroyed. They change the way they live and feed to fit in with their new homes. Some have done so well in cities that we now count them as pests.

City cliffs

In the wild, rock doves live and build their nests on cliffs and crags. Their cousins, the pigeons, live in many cities. They have found their own cliffs on the walls and ledges of city buildings. They feast on waste food and leftovers.

A town home

Creatures, such as mice, rats, squirrels, foxes, starlings, gulls, cockroaches and flies are a common sight in many towns and cities. In some countries, tree frogs and lizards have also made their home in towns. They even live in people's houses. Plants that now grow in cities include nettles, willowherbs, elder and buddleia.

Robins happily nest in quiet buildings or sheds.

City comforts

The city offers animals shelter, food and warmth. They shelter in roofs, walls and drainpipes and in corners of our warm houses. They feed on left-over food that we throw away in dustbins and on rubbish heaps. This is why so many animals do so well in cities. They change the way they behave and the food they eat so that they can use the things they find in the city.

In the roof

The roofs of churches, barns and other buildings are like giant tree houses for animals. They are used by animals all over the world:

- Raccoons in North America.
- Roof rats in Asia.
- Ring-tailed possums in Australia.

Did you know?

Some city animals become pests. Some cities have large numbers of pigeons which can spread diseases.

Useful rubbish

Animals quickly adapt to their new homes and diets. Raccoons, gulls and sometimes polar bears raid rubbish tips for food. Gulls also use rubbish to build their nests.

Gulls searching for food on a rubbish dump.

Glossary

adapted having special features that help an animal or plant survive in its habitat

algae simple plants that include seaweeds and tiny plants with only one cell

bacteria tiny living things that are found almost everywhere

barnacles tiny shellfish that cling on to rocks, whales and the bottoms of ships

breeding means producing new living things

bromeliads plants that grow high up on the branches of rainforest trees. They are related to pineapples.

camouflage having a special shape, colour or pattern that helps a living thing blend in with its surroundings

cell a tiny building block that makes up the body of all living things

chemical a substance found as a solid, liquid or gas

cold-blooded animals that cannot control the temperature of their bodies. They rely on the weather to warm them up or cool them down. They need to be warm to move about and search for food.

compete to struggle with something else

coniferous trees like pine trees that produce cones

dam a wooden wall made by beavers across a river or stream. It blocks off the river and forms a pond.

deciduous trees that regularly lose their leaves

dung an animal's droppings

estuary the end of a river where it flows into the sea

frond a feathery leaf or leaf-like part of a plant

gill part of a fish's body used for breathing in oxygen from the water

grasslands huge, open spaces covered in grass and bushes

habitat   a particular place where plants and animals live

hibernating   going into a deep sleep-like state for winter

holdfast   the round, root-like part of a seaweed that helps it cling to seashore rocks

larva   the young of an insect. A larva does not look anything like an adult insect.

lichens   living things that are a cross between algae and fungi. (Fungi include mushrooms, mildews and moulds.)

lodge   a wooden, dome-like home built by beavers

mammals   animals such as elephants, bats, horses and humans. They are the only animals that feed their babies on milk.

mate   a partner to breed with

migration   a long journey that some animals make to find a place with better food supplies or shelter

mites   tiny animals that are related to spiders

nocturnal   nocturnal animals sleep by day and come out at night to look for food

oxygen   a gas in the air. Living things need to breathe oxygen to stay alive.

poles   the two regions at the north and south ends of the Earth. They are the North Pole and the South Pole.

predators   animals that hunt and kill other animals for food

prey   animals that are hunted and killed for food

reproduce   to have children or young

reptiles   animals with scaly skin that live on land. They include snakes, lizards and crocodiles.

species   a group of living things that have certain features in common and can breed with each other

streamlined   having a smooth shape for cutting through the air or water

vicuña   a long, silky-haired animal that lives in the Andes Mountains

worm cast   a squiggle of sand on the seashore that is left behind by burrowing worms

Index

bacteria   27, 30

body parts   7

body shape   7

breathing   5, 16, 21

bush fires   26

camouflage   11, 23, 30

coasts and seashores
    18–19

cold and heat   6, 8, 9, 11,
    22, 23, 24, 25, 27

cold-blooded animals   6,
    30

colour and pattern   4, 7,
    11

competition   10, 30

deserts   24–5

extreme habitats   26–7

feeding   5, 14, 17, 19, 20,
    21, 23, 29

fish and shellfish   5, 14,
    15, 16, 17, 18, 19, 20,
    21, 23

forests   9, 10–11

grasslands   12–13, 30

habitats   4, 5, 6, 10, 14,
    20, 28, 30

hibernation   11, 30

insects   4, 8, 11, 13, 16,
    23, 25, 27

lakes and ponds   16–17

migration   11, 22, 31

mountains   5, 8–9, 27

movement   5, 7, 25

nocturnal animals   7, 31

oceans   20–1

plants   5, 7, 8, 9, 10, 11,
    13, 14, 15, 18, 22, 23,
    24, 26, 27

polar regions   22–3, 31

predators and prey   5, 6,
    11, 12, 17, 31

rainforests   9, 10

reproduction   5, 21, 31

rivers and estuaries
    14–15, 30

survival needs   5

towns and cities   28-9